Poems Against Death

POEMS AGAINST DEATH

Selected Poems of KARL KROLOW

Translations and Introduction by
Herman Salinger

Washington
The Charioteer Press
1969

THIS IS A *Charioteer Book.*

Library of Congress Catalog Card No. 71-82716

Published by The Charioteer Press, 601 19th Street, N.W., Washington, D.C. 20006.

Manufactured in the United States of America.

FIRST EDITION LIMITED TO 300 COPIES.

For Wendy, these translations:

filiae
anima in Arcadia consanguineae
d.d.
pater

ACKNOWLEDGMENTS

Several of these translations appeared in the anthology *Modern European Poetry*. The author makes grateful acknowledgment to Willis Barnstone, editor of the anthology, and Bantam Books, publisher.

Grateful acknowledgment is made also to Suhrkamp Verlag, Frankfurt am Main, Mr. Krolow's publisher.

CONTENTS

INTRODUCTION

In the midst of much flurry about and against "obscurity" in modern poetry, Karl Krolow wrote several years ago that "the poem has always been, by its very nature, incomprehensible." Its incomprehensibility is of the bred-in-the-bone variety. The modern poem is incomprehensible for those who fail "to bring sufficient sensibility and patience into their contact with it. Whether a hundred years ago or a thousand, the poem—in its sensitivity, its receptivity—has always been a few jumps ahead of what then was or what was about to come into being, ahead of each reader or listener." Krolow's examples of the precocity of the poem are surprising. He cites the writings of the Alexandrians, which now sound formal and conformist and seem the epitome of a poetic "establishment," and of the Spanish Baroque, the French Pléiade, and the Elizabethans. Young Goethe's lyrics were, says Krolow, as "revolutionary" to his contemporaries as Baudelaire's to his, as Rimbaud's and Mallarmé's to theirs. Now, is this not true down to Rilke and beyond? As Krolow's translator, I am very often reminded of the essential elusiveness (a form of pseudosimplicity) of William Blake, who so beautifully managed to convey and to conceal, to escape into uncaptured flight.

Why an introduction at all? Does Karl Krolow's poetry not speak for itself? Stand on its own feet? Indeed it does more than that; it flies, self-propelled and delicate, on swallow's wings, bat's wings, often with the green-and-yellow convolutions of leaves in wind. His *élan* is his own, spurting from deep layers of his labile sensibility. At the same time, we frequently become aware of something opposite: a built-in reserve that, while probably personal in its origins, forming a nearly equal reticence, yet has something peculiarly German and almost self-negating in it. His poems have the iron taste of deep, earthy well water but a saline aftertaste so subtle that we might miss identifying it as the taste of tears: his and our own, shed for no one particular cause: perhaps less for the human condition than for the fading beauty of a world wasting around us: hidden, occult, unobserved, and infinitely subtle and fallible. The beauty, if that is the word, is recondite because it is held together not by what Rilke would have called *Bezug* (pure relationship) but by some odd, at times whimsical, arbitrariness. This is none other than the apparent arbitrariness of Nature, and there—we have said it: Karl Krolow is a "Nature Poet": an often-made statement, I suppose, but one that we must nevertheless put forward and then immediately retract or at least stringently modify. He is generally genealogized as having "stemmed" from the modern school of German "Nature Poets" (*Naturdichter*), and the names of Oskar Loerke and Wilhelm Lehmann are cited as his forebears and "influences." That he stemmed from them may have a kernel of truth in it, but such a statement loses, by oversimplification, the real Krolow. "The Nature poem," to quote his own words, "became strangled by the chlorophyll-green jungle." He admits the need for detail in the nature lyric for the sake of the disburdening of the poet. He finds "the all too poetic reduced for the first time in our epoch." Regarding the need for "a dose of objectivity," he says that, "when the poem loses its breath, it tends to say 'eternity'." Krolow's style, like that of Paul Celan, has been "taken from the panorama of the human interior." To this he adds a playfulness, a lightness, at times a frivolity with words the aim of which is to destroy "intent." Hence Krolow's great mobility. "Playfulness must function or die," he states.

The signature of this poet is not to be found in rhyme scheme or form, not to be simplified out of his own wide activity as a translator from the modern French and Spanish poets (though one *feels* Verlaine or Lorca in him now and then). His characteristic signature is the nervosity of his sensibility, the lability of its expression, the work of the play instinct, at play with all the sacred toys of poetry: the word, the image, and the line, the blurred or doubled semantics. He plays a game of scorched earth in which the poem admittedly runs the danger of committing suicide. But, says Krolow, the poem is tough, hardy, resistant; it survives even the classroom exercises performed upon it. Finally, the present-day lyric is capricious—"and that is not the worst concession that one can make to a lyrical text." To read Karl Krolow is a pleasure. To translate him is to have partaken faintly and remotely of the internal, interior, inward experience behind each poem. I have tried to pass this on as purely as I can.

HERMAN SALINGER

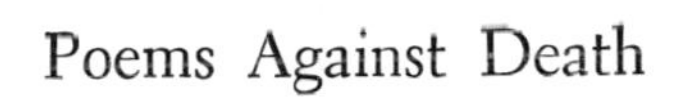

Poems Against Death

DEAD SEASON

It happened
that the ancestral portraits
fell from the wall
because it was so quiet.
The bottle of Beaujolais
united
with a few burst pears
into a still life.

It was the hour of the carp
and of the dying flies.

Afternoon blinked
under heavy eyelids.
Yet the sounds of the heart were
audible for a while
by the sailboat pond of the boys
who here, yesterday, had given out
their nautical commands.

Day before yesterday anyhow
everything had been different.
The dead season
still lived in the legend-light
smell of the grass.

Now they wait on the floor:
the broken pictures, waiting
for someone to step
out of the wall
and pick them up, laughing.

WHITE

White. A torn tablecloth.
Somebody swings it: white hand
of the eastwind.
Someone says: it's snowing.
Gradually
the torn air opens up
its eyes in the cold.

Snow is for writing.
One white letter long
time complies, smelling
of frost and apples,
till time melts.

WRITING

Paper, on which
a light wind settles.

Unpremeditated lines: waves
of a water that the hand
scoops from air, words
on my table like
pairs of lovers, bodies
of plants.

Paper: like fair weather,
to be written on,
forgetful as happiness,
garlands, hung withering
around the presence of death.

PORTRAIT OF A HAND

Five nailmoons rising
over the sky
of the right hand:

holding a black hair strand,
an ageless flower,
a nameless photograph.

The history of the ring finger
is not the history
of the index finger.

This hand grasped.
It slept the sleep
of its five moons
in another hand.

THE MURDERER

A pocketknife is enough
to kill the air
with her flying hair
and the memory of all names
left in her
unsuspectingly.

Stab. You will hit
the wind in its neck.
It will fall at your feet
as dust.

You raise your arm.
Soon you will be
the murderer
of your own breath.

MAGICIAN

In the cicadas
hides a magician
who sings.

He is young
as leaves and finches
that bewitch the ear.

The murmur of pitchers
echoing his voice.

With invisible hands
he shakes the noon's blue
in front of house doors.

By night he is the spy
in the blood of man and maid
before they get back
into their bodies.

Cicadas
find no sleep.

BEFORE MOWING

The world
is full of grass
for hiding women
and sudden fires
in.

Attempts
to keep one's breath
while it flutters
like a candle.

The sultry air
is a green animal.
Noon: a bundle
of tossed-off clothes,
time of
flower oracles.

Who dares
to speak
of the sharpness of sickles?

IT IS HOT

A basket of snails
sought shelter
in the poplar shade.

The vineyard women
long for the
cool bodies of lizards.

But they remain women,
fiery spice
in their eyes
with which they
can set
grainheaps afire.

Far off, the landscape
crackles: colored paper
somebody lighted.

The shadows are
the color of salamanders.

SOLITUDE

Je suis l'autre.—GERARD DE NERVAL

I

That dreamer, that middle-aged man:
he lets his hand fall out of the window
like a dustcloth.
He lets it go easily.
Without surprise he smiles after it
into a blueness etched with formic acid
and shows his decayed teeth.
He likes to be alone
with the limbs he has left.
His slender joints
still obey him for a while
as he listens into the sky,
while down below, the
young woman with the apron
bends over each single one
of the now-independent fingers
and slowly kisses them.

II

A quiet gleaming
came from him.
It was the light bulb
he had in his mouth.
Always in the twilight
its tender filaments
showed people the way
as they went past his building,
although he lived several stories up.
His hope was: to be noticed
as he walked up and down in his room,
lighting up the darkness
and feeling, between his gums and his tongue,
an indefinite longing for sociability.

One night there answered
at some distance
another light bulb.
He offered no resistance.
The silent competition
came too unexpectedly.
Since then electric light
falls without a shade from the ceiling:
ghostly shower, bathing a dead man.

III

The one neighbor he lets
play with his childhood,
the second with the accumulated
empty beer bottles.
He doesn't know either of them otherwise;
still, he would like very much to have them
take part in something of his
if they in return would occasionally greet him
mornings on the way to work,
evenings on the way from work.
He gives his past away,
year by year,
and spends the present
quietly with dice and with waiting
for everything to change
while a gold flame
hops out of the bunch of dry honeysuckle
that caught fire by itself
in front of his door.

IV

This arrest warrant
that moves along upright
enjoying its freedom,
which shares its meals
under the trees
with its willing anxiety:
roast meat, fruits, a liqueur—

He doesn't need any longer
to be alone.
He has a black bride around him
who takes all sorts of orders from him.

With him she buys
the tickets for the ghostly evening train:
a willing companion
with whom all day long
one shares meals under the trees.

Naturally he knows
that the night is the blue razor
with which she
unceremoniously
will cut his head from his body.

NIGHT'S BEGINNING

The night with the black pony-tail hair
looks into my eyes.
The river bathed her
a whole twilight long.
She showed herself to him
the way she was created.
Then she came
with light steps through the air
and her eyes
met mine.
The minutes were like cicadas
with delicate thighs.

I shall have to
lower my glances.

COUPLE

I

Narrow as wrists.

See our silent airplane,
child's kite,
no longer held
by fingers above a coast
where people now
are saying good night.

The carrier pigeon between us
climbs higher and higher.

We are in the beautiful house
without doors, sky,
unerasable blue
on our bodies.

II

The other life
with two pairs of eyes.

We have fever
like the stones
in the sun.

Still life of clothes tossed aside.

Our darkness—shining oil
poured uncertainly through the window.

In one common mouth
our breath flies away.

ELEGIES ON THE DEATH OF A YOUNG POET

For A. X. G.,
died September 14, 1952,
in Arles, Provence

I

Behind the woman's knee drawn up to her body, waiting
for the man,
the air—upright before the patterned curtain,
upright before the wallpaper lemonade
that slowly exudes into four corners;
behind the hotel room with the smell of central heating
and the slight wool of the shaved armpit hair,
with the view of the pine-tree slope and the crushed slate;
behind the quick breathing of two people in an embrace,
the five-minute noises of ecstasy in front of a mirror that's
watching,
as unparticipating as discarded underwear:

Behind all of this—

Behind the elastic rubber of time, the helpless moment of
life,
the tiny particle of October afternoon with flannel-colored
rain
and a trace of loose snow beneath clouds,
with fog that grips at the throat, inflames the tonsils
and makes the thoughts of the dead more tender;

behind the hovering arrack bottle
and the coin intended for the beyond, glistening at the
table's edge:

Behind all of this—

Behind the careful or casual today
that helps you into your overcoat and places the soup
plate precisely,
shielding against wind and sleeplessness:

Behind this and all this: your hectic shadow,
the ambiguous mobility of a ghost that would like to make
itself known.

Behind this and all: your mouth,
forming meaningless syllables, little calls, sounds from
beyond,
sounds from a land full of calm, edible dishes,
suitable for sea anemones and medusas . . .

You apparition on the slate slope,
without the grimace of sudden, self-dealt death,
with thin lips of eternity,
with lips fashioned out of new reason,
with eyes in whose corners the silence grew abstract
facing a landscape with flying fishes and hastily written
poems.
At twenty-nine you left,
to return as a whispering over a sloping berrypatch in late
autumn:

a dark lisping of agelessness swallowed up by evening,
as a mumbling between two hot showers in an overheated
bath.

Your face—halved by frustration—glistens.
It is the damp spot on the whitewashed wall,
turning liquid under the lazy ceiling light.

Your face behind the dark horn-rimmed glasses,
grown a thousand years old with strain
and gliding through the night that swallows shoulders,
loins, muscles:
night with snowfall of ashes from head hair and pubic
hair,
night with the chills of survivors before they pull the
covers up to their chins,
with cold thermal baths and distant salvos of guns,
Night, Night, Night . . .

Your handwriting, dissolved in paper serpentines, into
mottoed ribbons:
"You only live once" fluttering in the lovely, melancholy
wind,
pasted over your brow,
over your death-poisoned forehead.

—The world after your death holds no consoling Chinese
lanterns under your eyes.
It no longer knows anything about you in its twin-bedded
rooms
with the brandy that burns the gums and which
one feels in the circulation before love comes and goes.

It knows about you no longer. Therefore you appear
in vain. You are quite dead.
It is the recurrent rhyme for each of us at the last: quite
dead . . .

but perhaps
the movement of light and shadow that you made
remains:
the effort, the despair, the desperation,
short and violent joy, more strangely fragrant
than nectarines or than the flesh of pears.
Upswing, sweetly aromatic and more weakening than the
taste
of the fruit inside, suddenly burst open.
Perhaps the hard rhyme to guilt and guiltlessness that for
a moment
still stands in the destroyed air:
run dry already a moment later,
only a tiny crab in the web of loneliness,
happiness: a short interruption between torture and bore-
dom.

Perhaps even less than that is left—yet something;
for me: an apparition on the slate slope in Octobers
smiling before the twilights,
some insight into continued life amid much
that seems unbearable, seems hostile, too:

To live patient with objects and in the arms of phantoms,
of faith and love and hope; if necessary,
of this and that besides. Oh, in the arm

of an alder thicket, hanging over the water,
on it: a picture that looks like ourselves!
To live with the spirit that sets symbols, signs,
beneath a sky we cannot get beyond,
not even with jet bombers. . . .

II

The nightingale inside your head is silent,
the sobbing of an unknown bird,
the little throat in yours,
the voice above your voice.

She died because of you. Five deaths she died:
that of trust, that of hope, that of patience,
of love that outloves dejection,
and that of the human being you were, with passions,
with blood that rushes out of the bushes of night
into new night.

The unknown bird is silent: killed.
Its quick wingbeat, its fears
of you, of your grip, of your laying on of hands:
too late! The strange nightingale was buried in the air
in which you perished, in the zenith
of dreams that visited you readily
and daily. . . .
Her essence—more vulnerable than echo made of wind—
still lingers a little while in the memory
of silence as in an invisible cage.

She was a visitor in you,
come from the hinterland of life,
your life,
the guest from a creation (highly perishable)
full of chance and full of parable, superfluous
and useless as pressed algae, manes of grass, cicada spume.

The nightingale inside your head is silent,
the sobbing of an unknown bird,
the little throat in yours,
the voice above your voice.

Helpless, I strew winegrapes after her:
grapes blue, yellow, sweet crumbs
of silence.
Instead of beauty I feed nothingness,
with fool's gold, offal, or with mourning grief.
The nightingale inside your head is silent.
She died because of you, was killed by you.
And black wind purses lips to make his moan.

You are the killer of the unknown bird.

SLEEP

While I am sleeping,
the toy grows older,
held in a child's hands,
love changes its color
between two breaths drawn.
The knife in the doorpost
waits in vain
for a passerby
to plunge it into my breast.
Even murderers are dreaming now
beneath their hats.
A silent time: a time for sleeping.
You can hear the pulse of those
who want to remain invisible.
The wisdom of unspoken words
increases.
More warily now
the plants are blossoming.
There are no eyes now
to be astonished at them.

AWAKENING

Am I saying "Rose" for the first time?
Earlier I named
wrong names.
The minutes
my fingers enclose
have no weight.
When I feel it,
it will again be too late.
But now the day still has
just-opened eyes.
The night drew back
behind the lids.

POEMS AGAINST DEATH

I

The elongated fruits of the jasmine bush, pressed against
the breast,
hung with alchemistic mussel shells like ghostly play-
things,
and the sugar of the year's seasons on the lip—

Anima candida:
you stand straight before the sky and the wind,
catching innocent fishes by the wall,
the shadow of your own security in your arm.

On benches you sit in comfort.
The stubble does not prick your skin.
You are alive and show your teeth to the grapes
that hang down before your eyes.

But a dead man is not made of milk and blood;
and you will be like him
in the midst of wristwatches, which indicate the hour,
hour without an above or below,
without heaven and wind,
with soot in the fire, with a groaning into the blue night,
no longer calmed by barbiturates.

A dead man is no rhyme for tenderness.
A bundle of weeds on the flat palm of the hand
is clearer.

He still exists only
in lights they light for him,
in the unmade bed he has left,
in the smell that stayed with the woman when she was
through with him.
You will be like him.

II

A deck of cards the lyric landscape—easy to shuffle,
easy to hold in the hand in the dream
of green leaf-fingers.
And the one, the most worn card in the deck,
with the princes of this world in the picture,
over which no angels unfold themselves like sailboats—

death, unshuffled, marked with fear-sweat
and old laughter,
death with a leather-coat smell on the mahogany-painted
wall:
smoke before my eyes and already vanished again,
blown away into a confused landscape,
held by green leaf-fingers. . . .

III

Scratched into the angles of the horizon,
above the glowing places of rose and poppy,
above the heat in the flesh of invented fruits, the flesh of
life;
into the passing sweetness of an immature face, engraved
in it,

still with traces of night and man, on some morning,
lizard-cool and green-faced.
Scratched into the epidermis of the sky,
white as snow that tastes of the knife's edge:

your hostile image,
your invisible gestures and jokes,
with hands at the throat,
in ambush behind the bend of the tree-lined walk.

You pain in the left heart chamber
in the midst of perfect joy,
at the laugh of a seventeen-year-old mouth,
under eyes of fever and ice.

Closer than bodily closeness: you,
noise in the blood, no chatter of eternity
but the cruel singing of deathless gnats.

Above the glowing places of rose and poppy,
in a colored shirt that gleams through the bushes,
stripped off by a love that does not want to die:

your old countenance without color
terrible and lonely.

IV

Like birdswarm in the blue sea oats, a light cloud:
ill humour—a cloudbank—weakly at my two temples—

thus you are there, quite unexpectedly,
in a noon that is like a rising dolphin,
or evenings, smelling of tobacco smoke,
innocently between two pulse beats,
a slight murmur in my blood,
just while, forgetting, I let myself go in the game:

forgotten those leaves of the plane tree, bright-bellied as a
virgin,
forgotten the leaf-breath by night on the skin
in the wind that blew for strange soldiers,
forgotten the face of a woman, out of a Breton legend,
face bared by the lamplight,
as all is quickly forgotten and turns to light cloudwork.

Death, linnet light in the blue sea oats.

V

The sweet seeds of the early dawn
scatter through the thicket of the nightsky.
I can gather them up
and feel joy within me, like the wind,
the wind that has no fear of death.

The darkness has laid her head into her hands.
She gives way to the songbird swarm of ecstasy
That in me beats its wings.

Every morning speaks its verdict over death;
and the flight-smell of the night wafts away.

I seize time with my finger.
Time rests—a mobile dustgrain—in the cup of my hand:
perfect like the red sweetpea
that is hung with blossoms and with pods,
with the dry, split lip of the earth
that has been crossed by heat.

Existence is stronger now in the growing horn of the nails,
in the blond-and-black beard stubbles
and in women whose nipples stiffen under their blouses.

Every morning speaks its verdict over death.
The seeds of the dawn I have gathered up
and against the morning wind I sing:
Dead is Death!

VI

In a face the flickering of joy,
silent ship that sails out never to return home:

so evening comes.

Its life does not weigh heavy against the shoulder.
Gold cloud mass in arm, evening is there:
and once more death has patience:
a seer of ghosts whose own hide hates him
as long as the water aloes with white wombs blossom
and the twilight-dusk is light as a sandwasp.

Darkness trembles its lips:
beautiful, like the woman that doesn't exist.
Death it makes insecure, turns him a while away with its
whispering.

So evening comes.
Its life weighs lightly against the shoulder.

And night has the color of Jenny's eyebrows.
She is not like that friend who changes her perfumes.
She is not like that friend in whose eyes flits St. Elmo's
fire.
She has little teeth, little teeth that gleam.
She has a mouth of exultation and stillness.

And once more death has patience. . . .

WALK

Someone in the twilight is taking a walk
and singing.

The wolf from the fable
is in flight.

The wild plum thickets
hover before him.
The man in the moon
starts up out of the yellow straw
whenever anyone goes past.

The wind's hand rubs
the hazel nuts
whenever the darkness
likes anybody.

Somebody takes the night
upon his shoulders,
gives love her names,
and the hands of the dead
begin to stir again
in the dust.

GRAVESTONE FOR DOMENICO SCARLATTI

A hat in the air
is a bird
seeking its name
or the curtsy of frivolity
before all who remained on earth
without a piano.

A hat—a message
to heaven,
which harvested sonatas
when the fingers were sad
and forgot how to move.

A hat—for a while
it twitters from bright plumage.
Then it is slowly lost
in your light.

A LANDSCAPE FOR ME

I

In it
minerals and adjectives
collect.

Tree shadows permit
various descriptions.

Noon consumes
a fish
with geometric fin.

My landscape
makes one hungry as the wind.

Whoever has long arms
reaches to the sky.

Tired birds
sleep on the air.

Out of habit
hold
colored fruits in both hands.

Tradition of long twilights.

Night glows:
a heap of woodcoals.

II

The believable beauty
of a smokeplume.

Conscience
has the voice of an echo
on the horizon.

Quarter notes of a melody
from willowwood:

the excited sound
is lost like moth flight.

Surface of black olives,
arranged yesterday by Euclid.

Before my eyes
I let them
float in the dry light.

III

Above a salty shore
the mirroring of rowboats.

Smelling wet roses—
an announcement of death.

Crosspaths through green:
its silence
is untranslatable.

Plant pollen on my lids.

The fragile face of days
when foliage falls.
Carefully one bends
over leaves.

The suicide roses smell
of past poems.

BY THE LAKE

I

Let us go fish stones with cool faces
out of the lake
and throw them after the footsteps of those
who run away.
A shore is good, that the hook in the heart
be remembered and flowers
for the trout who died
be strewn
Let us go look for the eyes of the drowned
that glitter in the light of the embankment
and let us carry a little blue water
up toward the evening that soon
will sleep on the shore.

II

Do you understand that here nobody
is thirsty?
The tongue is moist with the taste
of friendly minerals
when you sit down in the shadow
of the beached boats, gently.
Only a breeze rises
and carries in its two hands
a bust:
the silence, without a mouth
that might whisper.

You will all rest this way
a long time,
until your likenesses,
headless,
will be carried away
by the tide.

III

We have washed off the anchor
each painted
on his breast.
We laughed that the heart of the current
never reached up to our necks.
One can no longer remain
captain of catfish.
Lake water clung for a while
to our soles. And the night
arrived as a siren.
Black her birdbody.

INSECT SEASON

Undiscoverable crickets
in the sultry air
like calls of shipwrecked men
in the blue summer water.

Insect season whirs
under great trees.

Cats devour goldfish
in the dry pond.

All plants grow
gothically into the rainless sky.

The humming nerves
of the high-tension wires.

ROBINSON

I

Again and again I stretch my hand
out to a ship.
With my bare fist I try
to grasp at its sail.
At first I caught
various vessels that
showed on the horizon.
I catch trout that way.
But the monsoon looked
at my fingers askance
and let them all go,
or oars and compass
broke. One must
handle ships gently.
For this I shouted names at them.
They always sounded
like mine.

Now I live only
in company with the disobedience
of a few words.

II

I have stopped counting,
even if I still have fingers
I can dip one after another
into the salty water.

Insects and tobacco leaves
do not know the time
I used to waste.

My last neighbor
who played the French horn
(he had once cleverly managed
to lift it from a folksong)
died at sea.

At times a little sun falls
on the table beneath which I stretch
my feet.
I do not need to have
longing any longer.

III

This habit of sitting a long time
on a chair somewhere
and listening: whether it is
raining inside oneself
or whether in the liver
the scorpion still stirs.

Counted are all the lightnings,
all the matchsticks that were left.

Till one has had enough of it
and drowns the very last
signal pennant
in the sea.

POET AND TRANSLATOR

Karl Krolow has influenced many of the poets of the new generation in Europe. A. Leslie Willson in *Dimension* attributes major importance to Krolow in the shaping of the character and quality of German poetry since 1945. Krolow has published about a dozen books of poems. He has also translated many of the Spanish and French moderns. Born in Hanover, Germany, in 1915, Krolow now lives in Darmstadt.

Herman Salinger has published eight books of his own poems and of translations of works by Rudolf Hagelstange and other German authors. Salinger's poems and his translations have appeared in leading magazines and in several anthologies. He was editor-translator of *Twentieth Century German* Verse: *A Selection* (Princeton University Press) and coeditor of *The Creative Vision* (Grove Press). Salinger is chairman of the Department of Germanic Languages and Literature at Duke University.

This book was composed on the Linotype
in Electra and printed by
Theo. Gaus' Sons, Inc., Brooklyn, N.Y. 11201